Disaster

SHIVERS

Disaster

by Terry Deary

WATTS BOOKS
London · New York · Sydney

© Terry Deary 1995

Watts Books

96 Leonard Street

London EC2A 4RH

Franklin Watts

14 Mars Road

Lane Cove

NSW

UK ISBN: 0 7496 2201 6

10 9 8 7 6 5 4 3 2 1

Dewey Decimal Classification 904

Editor: Rosemary McCormick

Designer: Mike Davis, Ian Probert

Author: Terry Deary

Cover Artist: Steiner Lund

Line Illustrator: Bob Harvey

Contents

The following titles are also available:

Mystery

Terror

Spooks

Introduction

If you fall downstairs it's an accident. But if a hundred people then trip over you and are crushed in the pile- up . . . that's a disaster.

If you fall downstairs, your unkind friends might laugh – it could have been worse, they say, it could have been them! But if a hundred people fall downstairs the world weeps.

This book looks at some true disaster stories and asks: "What is it like to be part of a disaster?" After all, the thing we are most interested in is ourselves. We want to know how we would behave if our life was in peril. Would we be courageous . . . or cowardly? This question can perhaps be answered by taking a look at how other people have reacted in such situations.

The stories here are of natural disasters like volcanoes and plagues and human-made disasters like crashes at sea, tragedies of war, fire and famine. The events are recounted from the point of view of someone personally involved. Some of the situations or conversations have been invented, but the facts behind everything you will read are true.

1. Plague — The Eyam woman

Memory can play tricks. A story can become twisted as people remember the unusual or the heroic. They forget the other side of the story. They forget that, in a disaster, some people never change. While a disaster brings out courage, it can also bring out greed, cowardice and cruelty. The people of Eyam are remembered for their goodness during the 1665-6 plague. But it wasn't quite that simple . . .

Eyam Village, Derbyshire – 1666

They call me "The Eyam woman" now. They look at me with suspicion. Children run away screaming when they see me in the street. Even older people keep as far away as they can when they pass me by. It's as if I'm a leper. I'm not. It's all because of what happened in Eyam back in 1666.

You probably know the story. It's famous. If you don't I'll repeat if for you . . . but I'll tell you the truth.

Eyam is a village up in the hills of Derbyshire. It's a dozen miles or so from the nearest large town. The middle of nowhere, you might say. But the lead mines brought work for the men and a village grew around that work. It's a village like ten thousand others. But Eyam became famous.

Of course the people of Eyam had heard of plagues in London. They say the city's dirty and dangerous. If the cut-throats and the footpads and the kidnappers don't get you, then the sickness will.

The last great sickness was in 1665. We had word of it – thousands dying every week – but we felt safe in our little village in the clean air of the hills. Maybe we were proud. Maybe that pride brought the plague as a punishment. Some of the women thought it was some other sin that made God angry. In the springtime some village boys had chased cattle into the church – the cattle left their droppings on the floor. The plague was sent as a punishment for that, they said. The boys are dead now, of course.

Some people said they saw the spirits of dead children flying over the village. Others saw white crickets sitting in their hearths. Sure signs of disaster. I saw nothing. Our farm stood on the hillside above the village. The first I knew of the disaster was when I went to church one September Sunday back in 1665 and the Rector, William Mompesson, climbed up to the pulpit with a worried face.

Mr Mompesson was a young man. He'd only been with us a year, but he had a lot of help from the old Rector, Thomas Stanley. Of course people forget Mr Stanley when they're talking about the heroes of

Eyam. It's always Mr Mompesson they think of.

That Sunday Mr Mompesson spoke in a slow, serious voice. "My friends," he said. "This week our village has been visited by a pestilence. Widow Cooper had taken in a tailor as her lodger. Some of you may have met him. His name was George Viccars. Mr Viccars had begun to sell clothes in Eyam and needed some more cloth. It seems a parcel was delivered from London some two weeks ago. You know about the plague in London. It is probable that this cloth contained the infection."

My six children grew restless beside me. "What's a plague, mamma?" Elizabeth asked me.

"Hush! Listen to the Rector," I said.

He went on, "George Viccars died. We mourned him and buried him. I am only sorry there was no money to buy a headstone for his grave. But in the past two weeks there have been six more plague victims. They were all neighbours of Mr Viccars. We thought we had buried the plague with the tailor . . . it seems we were mistaken. I know that many of you are afraid. I can only tell you to put your faith in the Lord and pray."

During prayers I looked around the church. There were six empty seats where the plague victims used to sit. But there were more than just those six. At the end of the service I asked Beth Hancock, "Where are the Bradshaw family?"

She gathered her children round her and whispered. "They've left the village. Run away. I wish we could do the same."

"They are rich," I said. "They can afford to leave

and set up a new home. We are tied to the farm. If we left it we'd starve."

"Aye," Beth Hancock said bitterly. "And if you don't leave it you risk the plague. The Lord punishes the sinners of Eyam – but not the rich sinners."

We returned to the farm, my husband John, me and the six children. I tried to tell them that the plague was just a sickness; I told them not to worry . . . that if they were good children they wouldn't catch it. My lies may have protected the children from the fear. It could not protect them from the sickness in the end.

As the winter grew colder the disease became weaker. Eighty people died before Easter of 1666. That was sad enough. Old friends; families we'd sold eggs and milk to; children that my family had known since they were born. All dead before Easter. How do you explain to your son that he'll never see his friend again this side of Judgement Day?

The thing that kept us going was knowing that it could have been worse.

In London the plague was finished. People began to return to the capital. In Eyam that May only four people died. The Bradshaws hadn't returned but the rest of us began to live life as normal.

Then, just we were sure we were safe from the clutches of Death, he returned. For Death doesn't die. That May he had only been sleeping a little while.

In June, Death breathed and blew away the people of Eyam like dandelion seeds in a gale. There was no resisting him. No herbs, no potions, no prayers, no charms could stop him. He swept away families and emptied houses. John and I thought of sending the children to my brother in Sheffield. But there were six of them. It was too much to ask.

Rector Mompesson's wife begged him to take her and their two children away. He said they could go without him, but he had to stay. In the end his wife Catherine stayed, but their children went. Don't ever forget that. In the dreadful six months that followed, Mompesson's children were safe in Doncaster.

That is when Rector Mompesson came up with the scheme that made him a hero in the land. First he closed the church. We believed that standing closer than three paces to a plague victim could infect you. Victims carried the bad air with them. It would be foolish to bring the sick and the well together in the church.

He told us all to meet at a spot called Cucklett Delph, a sheltered hollow with a stream running through it. We stood in family groups, not daring to come too close to other families. Rector Mompesson climbed onto a rock and told us what he wanted us to do. "The village of Eyam has been visited by the plague," he said. "We have faced it bravely until now and borne our sufferings with courage. However, we have a duty to others outside of our village. We cannot risk carrying this dreadful infection to other towns. I would ask you to stay in the village for however long it takes. Do not leave Eyam while there is the chance that you might carry the plague with you."

It was to be a death sentence for many of the people gathered in Cucklett Delph. "How will we eat?" my husband asked. "Eyam does not produce enough of its own food. We need to get to market."

The Rector nodded. "The Earl of Devonshire who owns much of our land has offered to provide for us. If there is anything else we need then it can be left at the village boundary. We can leave the money at the boundary marker stone. I have had a hollow carved in the stone. It will be filled with vinegar. We will leave money in the vinegar so the collector will not catch the disease."

"What if we choose to leave?" someone asked.

"Then there are guards on the road. You will be brought back." He looked around the silent crowd and said. "Remember, our Lord died so others might live. We in Eyam can do no less. Any one person leaving will betray the rest of the village."

I'll swear he was looking at me when he said that. Perhaps it was my conscience – escape was exactly what I had been thinking of.

"I have one more thing to say," Rector Mompesson announced. "We have lost two grave-diggers and the church can no longer help you to bury your dead. Each family must in future bury their own dead. In their gardens, in the orchards or in the fields. There will be no church services for them, but Rector Stanley and I will say prayers. Each Sunday we will hold the usual services, but we will hold them here. May God be with you," he finished, and left us to walk the lonely path back to our farm. Our prison.

I went with the children each day to the village with eggs and milk for sale. I exchanged news with the other women. We talked about the latest victims . . . and every time the talk came around to escape. "I would kill anyone who tried to flee from Eyam,"

Sarah Carter said. Again I felt the shame of my own guilty thoughts and turned away.

I do not want to tell of August 1666, but I suppose I must. Seventy people and seven died in that dreadful month. I'm sorry, I cannot care about the seventy. I can only care about the seven. My seven.

The children grew bored on the farm and went into the village to play. Those they played with died within a week. After two weeks my son Edward complained of a fever. He sneezed. A red rash appeared on his skin. Purple lumps swelled painfully under his arms. He died. But even while my husband buried him, William, Alice and Anne fell sick. On 7th August my husband buried all three in shallow graves in the field below the house. Elizabeth followed two days later. Henry and Charles followed on 10th August.

I had cried when the first of my children died. I had no tears left for the last. My husband and I had the fever on 12th August. I lay down and waited to die. I welcomed Death like an old friend who would unite me with my children. I fell asleep that night and hoped I'd never wake in this life.

But I did. As my husband breathed his last breath the next morning I grew stronger every minute. Some people did get better in Eyam that summer – and those who did were safe from ever catching the plague again.

I was one of the unlucky ones who lived.

I wandered into the village hardly knowing where I was going, or why. That was when I met Marshall Howe, a foul-smelling, grey-skinned miner.

"Good day, Mrs Taylor," he said. "How are the

family?"

"Dead, Mr Howe, all dead."

"Sorry to hear that, Mrs Taylor. If you need any help, just let me know."

"Help?"

"Burying your loved ones. I've set up in business as a grave-digger. I only charge a sovereign a grave," he said.

"My husband . . ." I said.

"You want him burying?" he asked with a strange and ghoulish joy.

What could I do? I led the way back up the hill and he chatted happily. "Terrible times, Mrs Taylor," he said. "My wife and son have just died. Still, life must go on."

"Why?" I asked.

He chuckled and said, "It's a busy time for me. To keep up with the work I'm digging graves while the sick are still breathing. Hah! The other day I almost buried one while he was alive! James Unwin, my neighbour, in fact. He was almost gone so I dug his grave and went to collect him. Tied a bedsheet round his ankles and dragged him out of the door. He suddenly sat up and asked for water! Just in time! He's getting better now!" The man laughed. I felt sickened . . . but not by the plague. He talked on.

"Have you heard about Margaret Blackwell? She fell ill last week and her brother had no hope for her. He cooked himself some bacon for breakfast and poured the fat into a jug before he left for work. Poor Margaret woke up with a feverish thirst and grabbed the jug of warm fat. She drank it back, thinking it was milk. It made her sick, of course, but the miracle was it cured her! I've been trying to sell that bacon-fat idea as a plague cure myself. Well, a man has to make a living, doesn't he?"

I didn't answer. We reached the farm and I left him to bury my John. He came to the door half an hour later for his money. "For another sovereign I'll make sure you are buried when your turn comes," he said.

I closed the door on him. The house was quiet. No more sighing and crying of the sick. Only the ghosts of my family. So many, so short a time.

I couldn't milk the cows and herd the sheep and cut the hay all by myself! I needed help. I'll swear that was all that was on my mind when I walked out.

I didn't go by the road. I went over the hills and reached Tideswell later that afternoon. There were guards on the road to the town. "Where are you from?" the man asked.

"Orchard Bank," I said, and that was true. It was the place where I'd buried my family.

"Where's that?" he asked.

"In the land of the living," I said and walked past him.

It was when I asked a woman the road to Sheffield that she looked at me closely . . . and screamed. She'd recognised me. We'd sold our lambs to her at Tideswell market. "Eyam woman!" she shouted. "Eyam woman!"

In moments I was in the centre of a swirling mass of hatred. People threw vegetables, sticks, mud and stones at me till I was driven all the way back to Eyam.

Their hatred was bad enough. The hatred of the Eyam villagers was worse. I was the traitor who had let them down. I was the one who did what they only dreamed of doing and escaped.

When winter came the plague finally left Eyam. At last they opened the roads and I went to stay with my brother. I'm there now.

The Rector Mompesson became a hero. His wife died of the plague . . . and I'm truly sorry for that . . . but his children lived. Mine didn't.

Even the vile Marshall Howe is respected in his village. I am despised wherever I go.

I am "The Eyam woman". I am the traitor. I am the unforgiven.

Why?

The Eyam woman — FACTS

1. Rector Mompesson was offered a job in another part of the country. He married again and began a new life at Eakring in Nottinghamshire in 1670. Mrs Taylor would have been surprised to discover that he was not welcome in his new home. People still worried that he might be carrying the plague . . . even though the last death had been four years before! For a long time they did not want to come to his house or to his Eakring church.

2. Some people survived the plague by leaving their house and living in the fields beside Eyam. One man who had lost his whole family took only a cockerel for company. He survived many months. Finally he awoke one morning to find the cockerel had deserted him. When he went back to his old house he found the cockerel waiting there . . . and news that the plague had finally ended. It seemed the cockerel knew before he did!

3. In 14 months nearly 260 Eyam villagers died from the plague. Many must have departed before the ban on leaving was enforced. Eyam's Sheldon family fled to safety on the other side of the hill and took all their livestock with them . . . but their ducks flew home to Eyam pond! Rector Mompesson's decision to cut the village off may well have saved lives in other towns. But it was not as new an idea as many people seem to think. In fact, lots of little

communities risked their lives in this way to prevent the plague from spreading. Eyam was the last to do so and the story has been told many times. However, it was not the only plague village.

4. Eyam village today is a tourist attraction. Many of the old cottages still stand, with plaques to say who died in the plague. Many descendants of the plague families still live in the village. There are tours to the grave sites and the border-marker with the hollow for coins can still be seen. The only plague victim to be found buried in the churchyard is Mompesson's wife, Catherine. Every year the wife of the present Rector places roses on the grave in her memory.

5. Where did the plague first come from? In October 1347 a fleet of ships struggled into Messina harbour in Sicily. There were few sailors left to sail them properly, and those sailors were sick and dying. The harbour masters looked at them in horror and ordered them not to come ashore. The people of Messina didn't want to catch the sickness that the sailors brought from the east. So the men stayed on the ships and one by one they died. But they had thrown ropes onto the quayside and tied up their ships. Rats scuttled along the ropes and ran ashore. The rats carried fleas. Those fleas bit into their hosts and sucked their blood. They left behind a dreadful germ that made the rats ill. The dying rats hid in human homes, under the straw of beds and in the hay in stables. When the rat was

dead the flea looked around for a new host. The first human to lie in the straw or lift the hay was a perfect new victim. The flea bit the human as it had the rat. The human became ill and died a painful fevered death. In fact, the rats were carrying a bacteria called Yersinia pestis.

6. By June 1348 the plague had reached Paris. That summer it also crossed to England and spread its terror there. People knew it was coming their way . . . but didn't know how they could stop it. It was six hundred years before they discovered that the rats and their parasites were the cause.

7. The plague in 1348 killed almost half of the people in England. It returned several times over the years but never quite so destructively as that. Historians call that attack "The Black Death" because of the way the victims' skins were covered with deep purple blotches. The other famous epidemic came in 1666 and became known as "The Great Plague". This brought fear and suffering mainly to London. Still no one suspected the fleas.

8. Those fleas could live for 80 days without a host. This meant they could hide in the goods that tradesmen carried around the country. The Eyam plague almost certainly sprang from a bundle of cloth that a tailor brought into the village. The tailor was the first to die.

9. *In the 14th Century, people did not know how to control the disease. Doctors tried all sorts of remedies. Sometimes the cure was worse than the illness. For example, they cut open boils and inserted red hot pokers. Doctors thought this might clean the infection.*

2. War — Empire heroine

As if accidents and natural disasters aren't deadly enough, humans arrange to kill each other in large numbers. They start wars. And, in these wars, women and children are also under threat from the enemy. In the first Afghan war the British faced an even deadlier enemy than the Afghan rebels . . . the stupidity of their own army commanders!

Afghanistan – 1842*

The young woman wore a white dress and a wide-brimmed hat. It sheltered her eyes from the glare of the sun in a cornflower-blue sky. She sat on the balcony of the Indian hospital and looked towards the purple Himalayan mountains in the distance. Her feet and hands were bandaged but she was in no pain.

A man stepped onto the balcony. He was sweating inside a tight black suit, stiff-collared shirt and bowler hat. Sweat was making his large brown moustache

23

*The place and year of the battle and retreat

glisten in the afternoon heat. "Mrs Charlotte Carmichael?" he asked, taking off the bowler hat nervously. "It is a pleasure to meet a heroine of the British Empire!"

She turned her head slowly and glared at him. "Mr Arthurs, I presume, from the *London Times* newspaper? Excuse me if I don't shake hands." Her voice was crisp and her tone sharp. She was not a woman to suffer fools gladly.

"No excuse is necessary. Talking to you is a great enough honour," the reporter said with a polite bow.

"You have come all this way just to interview me? I am the one who is honoured," she said – but she seemed to be mimicking his style.

"You have a remarkable story to tell," the man said, resting the hat on a table and sliding into a seat next to her. "Sixteen thousand people dead and you are the only survivor. It's a miracle!"

She looked at him with steady, green eyes. "It was a disaster, Mr Arthurs. You should not be telling the story of one living woman. You should be telling Britain about the deaths of the others. Unnecessary deaths, I might add."

"I will write whatever you wish to tell me, Mrs Carmichael."

"Good. Then begin with the story of the British invasion. How we sent an army to occupy Afghanistan. No one asked the Afghan people, of course. Naturally they objected and fought to drive us out!"

"May I ask how you came to be here?" the reporter enquired, slipping a pencil and a notepad from his jacket pocket.

"I was with my husband, Major Alex Carmichael. Most of the officers had their wives with them on this expedition. They thought it would a be a safe little invasion. The Afghans weren't prepared for us in 1839 and we didn't meet much resistance. By August 1840 we'd taken the capital, Kabul, and it seemed too easy. Wives and children came out to settle with the army. God knows why we Brits should want to live in Afghanistan! Three quarters of the country is mountain and a lot of the rest desert. Let the Afghans have it, I say."

"I think Queen Victoria has ideas of a greater empire . . ." the reporter began.

"Queen Victoria isn't risking her fat little neck to get it. She leaves that to her soldiers," she snapped. "First she allows poor old General William Elphinstone to command the army in Afghanistan! Willie Elphinstone!"

"General Elphinstone had a great record," said Mr Arthurs defensively.

"Yes! He fought bravely . . . in the Battle of Waterloo. In eighteen-hundred-and-fifteen! Twenty-five years ago. By the time he got here he was a wreck. Pass me a medical dictionary and I'll mark the few diseases he didn't have. It's easier. The poor dear had gout and rheumatism and his arm in a sling. He couldn't walk and he couldn't ride. He had to be carried everywhere in a chair, for goodness sake. And, I'm sorry, it has to be said . . . his mind was becoming rather weak! This was the man in charge of 16,000 British and Indian lives in Kabul."

"He had Brigadier John Shelton to assist him," the reporter said.

"Hah! That man!" Charlotte Carmichael exploded. "A bad-tempered bully. Willie Elphinstone and Johnny Shelton hated each other. Did you know that Shelton went to the planning meetings with a bed and a quilt? He lay down, pretended to fall asleep and snored all the way through."

"I don't think reports of that have reached the press," Arthurs said coldly. This was not the story his readers wanted to hear. "General Elphinstone still led the Councils of War, though, didn't he?"

"They were a comedy, Mr Arthurs. Anyone who fancied coming along dropped in on the meetings. Junior officers insulted senior ones. Everyone argued while Shelton snored on the floor. I even called in and gave advice myself from time to time. Told them about the fortress for a start."

"That's right, there was a fortress built for the troops outside of Kabul city, wasn't there? It seems like a good idea – keep the fighting and the soldiers outside the city!"

"Good idea!" Charlotte Carmichael groaned. "I shall tell you what I told them. It was madness."

Her sore and cracked fingers poked out from underneath the bandages as she counted off the points. "*One*: they built it on a low area of swampy ground. The mountains were all around. The Afghans could sit in the mountains and fire down on the fortress. Lots of soldiers were shot inside the place. *Two*: the walls around the fortress were two miles long. We couldn't defend that length of wall properly.

26

The men were too spread out. And *three*: the camp supplies were a quarter of a mile from the fortress – outside the walls! All the Afghans had to do was capture the supply depot and wait for the British army to starve to death."

"What happened when the Afghan rebellion began?"

"First Kabul and our fortress were cut off. The Afghans closed the roads back to India. We got messages through asking for help. The reply was that it was too dangerous. We were on our own. They said Willie Elphinstone would organise our defence. He organised it so badly that the Afghans marched into Kabul, murdered the British Governor and all his staff while the army sat outside in its fortress! Then of course the Afghans turned on our fortress. Just as I predicted, they attacked the stores depot. We had to watch while the Afghans stole our food and drink supplies. We only had enough inside the walls for three days."

"And after three days?"

"After three days the officers begged General Elphinstone to let them go out to attack the Afghan fighters. Old Willie said he'd think about it! Then he had one of his good days. He felt fit enough to sit on his horse."

"The General led his men out into battle?" Arthurs asked excitedly. This was a terrific story.

"I didn't say that," Charlotte corrected him. "I said he sat on his horse."

"And then?"

"And then he fell off the other side. Silly old fool,"

she snorted and shook her head. "A bit unlucky, mind you. While Willie was trying to get up, the rotten animal stepped on his leg."

"That was tragic."

"It would have been more tragic if he'd tried to ride into battle," the woman sniffed. "Anyway, I think it affected his head. He decided to announce they were short of ammunition. They couldn't attack, he said. They should try to make peace with the enemy."

"But the Afghans wouldn't talk?" the reporter asked.

"No! The British wouldn't talk! Insufferable Shelton told Willie they had enough ammunition for 12 months. Then he ignored the General's orders and set out to attack the enemy."

"That was brave," Mr Arthurs said.

Charlotte rose painfully to her feet. "Shelton was a nasty brute of a man – but he wasn't a coward."

"So he drove the enemy back?" the reporter asked. He was desperate for a tale of a brave British action to take back home. Mrs Carmichael's story was not that. In fact, his newspaper would not even publish a story of such a bungling, amateur army.

"My husband was there and he told me the details. Oh, how we laughed!"

"Laughed?"

Charlotte limped from the rail of the balcony and began to walk through the action as she described it. "Ah, yes. It was rather funny. Shelton's men lined up with muskets loaded. The Afghans rode down from their mountain camp and charged the British line. 'Hold your fire, men, until I give the order – then

28

shoot to kill!'" she cried, acting the part of Shelton. "The Afghan horsemen came closer and closer . . . still gallant Shelton held his fire. At last they were so close the musketeers couldn't miss!"

"And then?" Arthurs asked excitedly. This was the stuff his readers wanted.

"And then . . . the smoke cleared. The British saw that not one horse or enemy soldier had been hit. Not one! Our troops looked very smart in their uniforms, you understand. Unfortunately they were rotten shots. They were so busy building forts and marching about that they never took the time to practise useful little skills like firing a musket!" she said.

"What happened next?" the reporter asked. He'd dropped his pencil now in despair and watched Charlotte as she limped around the table.

"Imagine, enemy horsemen riding round you, threatening to cut you to pieces. Your musket is empty. What do you do?" she asked dramatically.

"Re-load and fire again," Arthurs said quickly.

"Exactly what Shelton told them to do," the woman nodded.

"And they did?"

She sighed heavily. "And . . . they didn't. They decided to run away. Ran back to the camp like bolting rabbits, I'm afraid. Shelton had no choice but to run after them."

"British soldiers do not run away, Mrs Carmichael," Arthurs said stiffly. "They 'retreat'. Only cowards run away."

"Mr Arthurs, throwing your weapons away and racing back to the fortress cannot be described as a

29

retreat. They ran away! But at least they lived to fight another day. Remember, my husband was among those men you are calling a coward!"

Arthurs turned red and sweat began to run from his forehead to his collar. "Mrs Carmichael," he said quietly, "I'm so sorry."

"It doesn't matter. My husband had the choice of being a vicar or joining the army. If he'd chosen the church he'd be alive today. Poor Alex. Courage was not his strong point," she shrugged.

"I see," Arthurs blinked. "Was that when General Elphinstone ordered the retreat from Kabul?"

"Lord, no! Shelton wanted another crack at the enemy. He ordered another attack. He came up with a different plan of action. This time they took a cannon with them. Instead of forming a line they formed a square."

"Like the Battle of Waterloo. That would be much better," Arthurs nodded.

"Much better for the Afghans, yes," Charlotte said. "A much better target, you see? The Afghans changed their plan as well. They didn't charge this time. They simply fired their muskets at the packed square of men. The enemy were very good shots – lots of practice, you see – and with the British so crowded together they could hardly miss. That's when my husband was hit."

"I'm sorry," Arthurs repeated sincerely.

"Don't be, Mr Arthurs. It was a better death than the others suffered," she said, looking at her bandaged hands. "They may even give him a medal."

"So the cannon didn't keep the Afghans away?"

"Of course it did – so long as it was working. Trouble was, it became too hot. The gunners had to leave it to cool down. When the cannon went silent the enemy attacked. Our soldiers shot and our soldiers missed again. Some of the officers even tried to throw stones at the Afghans to drive them back! In the end the British . . . er . . . 'retreated' again."

Arthurs stroked his moustache thoughtfully. "I could, of course, praise the skill and nobility of the gallant enemy," he said.

"Skill and nobility!" the woman cried. "Lady Sale watched the whole calamity from the walls of the fort. She recognised some of the gallant enemy. They were shopkeepers and labourers from Kabul. Tell the British public the truth, Mr Arthurs. Willie Elphinstone was not fit to command – and the men weren't fit to fight. They should never have been in Kabul in the first place."

Arthurs shook his head. "General Elphinstone is a hero. He was buried with full military honours. He was wounded in the fighting!"

Charlotte Carmichael sat down heavily. "He was shot," she admitted. "I suppose the army didn't tell you where?"

"No, they didn't."

"He was hit in the backside," she said.

Arthurs blinked. "Oh, I say, Mrs Carmichael. I can't publish that."

She shrugged. "And I suppose you can't write too much about us leaving Kabul, can you?"

"It was a brave attempt to retreat to safety," he said.

She shook her head very slowly. "It was suicide.

31

Have you seen those mountains in winter?"

"I've never been to Afghanistan," the reporter admitted.

"Those mountains are very high. The only way to travel is through the passes. The lowest pass is 10,000 feet. Mr Arthurs, the highest mountain in Britain is Ben Nevis. It is not even 5,000 feet. We had to climb twice the height of Britain's highest mountain, carrying food and children. It was January and the snow was over a foot deep. People were dying of the cold before we even reached that dreadful pass. Of course the Afghans knew that. They simply waited for us in the Khyber Pass and attacked. It wasn't war, Mr Arthurs, it was a massacre."

The reporter was horrified. "Women and children, Mrs Carmichael. That's not fair."

Charlotte looked towards the distant mountain. "We were so wrapped in blankets the Afghans didn't know who they were attacking. They were just trying to drive invaders from their home land. I was hit with the butt of a rifle and left for dead. When I awoke I found a few Indian soldiers alive and they helped me finish the journey safely." She held up her hands. "I am lucky that I only suffered frost-bite."

"And do you feel bitter, Mrs Carmichael?"

She turned her sharp, green gaze on him. "Oh, yes, Mr Arthurs, I feel bitter. Bitter towards that fat little queen sitting on her safe throne back in London. To her ministers who send doddering old idiots like Elphinstone to lead fools and cowards to the ends of the earth. Sixteen thousand dead and for what?"

"I can't write that!"

"Then people back in Britain will never know the truth," she said. "You can share the blame if it happens again. Would you like that, Mr Arthurs?"

Before he could reply she had turned her back on him and was limping back into the hospital.

Empire heroine — FACTS

1. The British reported that only one person survived out of the 16,000 who crossed from Afghanistan to India. In fact, some Indian soldiers lived to tell the tale . . . but the British didn't consider that they mattered enough to count them as survivors.

2. In fairness to Major General William Elphinstone, when he was offered the Afghanistan job he said he was too old and sick to take it. The Governor General of India, Lord Auckland, knew that Elphinstone was not fit for the job, but still insisted that the old man should be placed in charge. If there is any one person to blame for the disastrous expedition, then Lord Auckland is perhaps the prime candidate.

3. Elphinstone was also not entirely to blame for walking into the Khyber Pass ambush. Before Elphinstone began the retreat, the Afghan army promised the British a safe passage back to India. However, the tribes in the mountains probably did not know about the agreement and attacked anyway.

4. Elphinstone died early in the retreat, before the massacre in the Pass. His body was recovered and carried in a coffin down the mountain. But he wasn't allowed to rest in peace. The escort was

attacked, the coffin torn open and Elphinstone's body pelted with stones. Eventually another expedition recovered the body and Elphinstone was buried . . . a British hero!

5. *The British invaded Afghanistan to keep the Russians from entering the country. Strangely, the Russians did occupy Afghanistan . . . in the 1980s. But, like the British a hundred and forty years before them, they couldn't defeat the mountain tribes. In the winter of 1989 the Russians withdrew all their troops; 118,000 Russian soldiers returned home fairly safely . . . but they had the help of helicopters. Old William Elphinstone didn't.*

6. *The British army has an unfortunate history of brave soldiers being led to their death by ignorant officers. They have been described as "lions led by donkeys". Yet Major General William Elphinstone does not qualify as the worst military leader of all time. That accolade could easily go to General Sir William Erskine, who had twice been resident in a lunatic asylum before he was given command of the British army during the Napoleonic wars in the early 1800s. In addition, Erskine's eyesight was so bad that his officers had to point him in the direction of the enemy. At the battle of Sabagul he managed to send his soldiers the wrong way and let the French enemy army escape. At the siege of Almeida he wrote an order instructing his men to defend a bridge against the enemy. He put the order in his pocket . . . then forgot about it. He found the*

note as he undressed for bed eight hours later. By the time he had passed it on to Colonel Bevan it was too late. The enemy had crossed the bridge and escaped easily. Erskine blamed Colonel Bevan for arriving too late!

3. Famine — Road of funerals

It's curious how disasters are often linked. Some links are obvious – an earthquake, for example, may kill hundreds, and then many thousands more may die when a huge ocean wave, caused by the earthquake, swamps coastal towns. Other links are less obvious. From 1845–1848 the British government was concerned with the wars in Afghanistan and India. They were so worried about events like the retreat from Kabul that they ignored an even greater disaster in a part of their own country: Ireland.

Ireland – 1845-48*

"History is boring," moaned Ian, throwing his school bag on the settee and switching on the television. "The Irish Famine! I ask you! Mrs Mallam asked us to do notes on the causes of the Irish famine! The potatoes all went bad and the Irish starved," he moaned. "What else is there to say?"

*The period in Irish history which saw great hardship due to famine

"Want some help?" said his sister Laura turning from her computer in the corner of the room.

"Do you know anything about the Irish Famine?" asked Ian.

"No."

"Well, how can you help?"

"I've got the computer here and an Encyclopedia disc. Want me to look it up for you?"

"Suppose so."

"Well, don't go mad with gratitude," she said.

"I won't," he promised.

"Here you are," Laura said as she clicked at the computer. The printer whirred and the report slid out.

In the first half of the nineteenth century the population of Ireland rose steadily. It grew from 5 million in 1800 to 8.2 million in 1845.

"So what?" Ian asked.

"So . . . famine means you don't have enough food for the people – or it could mean you have too many people for the food. In Ireland they may have had both problems together."

Laura read on . . .

"After the end of the Napoleonic Wars in 1815 the Irish soldiers were sent home to earn a living. There were not enough jobs so families were forced to scrape a living from a small patch of rented land."

"So the Napoleonic wars were another reason for the famine? What does it say about the potatoes?" her brother asked, scribbling notes in his jotter.

"Most of the peasants had just an acre of land. They grew potatoes on it. Most families had a house cow. They made buttermilk from it and mixed it with the potatoes. This was their main diet."

"Couldn't they buy other things to go with it?" Ian asked.

"Hang on . . . it says here that any extra money they raised had to go towards the rent on the land. Most of the landlords lived nowhere near the land. They just seem to have collected the rents. Men like the Earl of Lucan."

"The one who tried to murder his wife?" Ian asked.

"No," Laura said. "That was Lord Lucan in the 1970s – probably one of the Earl's successors."

"So tell me about the Earl of Lucan," Ian said.

"I'll find him on the disc. You be having a look at the rest of the information on that print-out."

In 1845 a potato disease spread from North America. It was a type of fungus which flourished in wet weather. The early summer had been fine and warm, but August 1845 was especially wet in Ireland. Nonetheless the potato crop looked excellent. Then suddenly there were reports from all over the country.

Potatoes looking fine when they were dug up but turning black and giving off a terrible smell when they were cooked. No one could eat them.

"Sounds like school dinners," Ian muttered to himself.

Laura sighed. "It's fine for you to make fun of someone else's problems. But if your main food supply was cut off you'd pretty soon start moaning."

"I'd get my food somewhere else," he argued.

"No potatoes meant no spare money. No money means no other food. You'd have starved." She pulled a sheet from the printer and scanned it quickly. "And that's not your only problem."

"What do you mean?"

Laura read out: "The Earl of Lucan. The Earl from County Mayo, Ireland, is best remembered for his part in the Charge of the Light Brigade in 1854. He is remembered as a hero in the poem 'Charge of the Light Brigade' by Alfred Tennyson. However, during the Irish Famine he was notorious for evicting 40,000 Irish peasants from the land they rented from him."

"Evicting?" Ian asked. "You mean they had no money so he threw them out?"

"That's it," Laura agreed. "Now they had no food, no chance of earning more from the land . . . and no home, of course."

"Some hero," Ian grumbled.

"We're studying Tennyson in Year 11," Laura said, pulling a poetry book from her school bag. She flipped through the pages and rested her finger on a paragraph. "Here you are. It seems Alfred, Lord Tennyson thought the great Lucan was doing the Irish a favour!"

She cleared her throat before reading from the book: "The Irish are all furious fools. They live in a horrible island and have no history of their own worth any notice . . . Couldn't someone blow up that horrible island with dynamite and carry it off in pieces – a long way off?"

"Charming!" Ian sighed. "Anything else?"

"There's something here about the Corn Laws of England. They made it very hard for small farmers to make a living. The Irish had to send some of their best corn and animals over to England," Laura said, turning away from the computer. "There you are, that's your homework done. The causes of the Irish Famine. Soldiers coming from the war were forced to live on the land. They grew mainly potatoes because the Corn Laws were so harsh. When the potatoes were diseased the families starved and were thrown off their land. Is that enough?"

"No!" Ian objected. "I want to know what happened next! Didn't anyone try to help?"

His sister turned back to her keyboard and tapped in some new commands. "Here's something on the effects of the famine: 'Thousands of Irish peasants died in their homes from starvation. Ships full of corn and cattle were taking the Irish food across to England while the Irish tried to live on nettles, plant roots and even grass. Many families were evicted and died of exposure or diseases like cholera and scurvy. They fell in the ditches by the side of the roads. The survivors tried to bury their dead in shallow graves but the bodies were dug up and eaten by hungry dogs.'"

Ian whistled softly through his teeth. "That's the sort of history teachers never tell you!"

"Hang on," Laura said tapping furiously. "It says, 'see *The Black Prophet* – a book by William Carleton.' You can read what Carleton wrote from the screen, if you're interested."

Ian moved over to the computer and peered with interest at the words on the screen:

The roads were literally black with funerals and, as you passed from parish to parish, the death bells were ringing forth in slow and gloomy tones. They were ringing a triumph of Death over the face of our

41

devoted country – a country that was filled with darker desolation and deeper sadness every day.

"Couldn't they have gone somewhere where there was food?" the boy asked.

"They went to America. Hundreds of thousands of Irish crossed the Atlantic," Laura said, scanning the screen. "The trouble was they could only afford passages on old, leaky ships. Many of the ships sank and the passengers drowned . . . or they were so crowded that thousands died of disease before they even reached America. And the ones who did get there weren't welcome. The Canadian and the US governments put them in camps but there were just too many people. 20,000 died of disease and starvation on the journeys – then more died in the camps. The ones who were let out found that no Americans wanted to give them work. Signs went up saying 'No Irish need apply'."

"That's racist," Ian said.

"It would be today," Laura nodded. "There were no laws against it in those days."

"Mrs Mallam said Ireland was part of Britain in 1845. Didn't the government try to help?"

Laura tapped away and grinned. "Thought history was boring," she said quietly.

"This is about people – not dates and battles and things," Ian argued.

"Here we are, then," Laura said. She pointed to the screen.

The British Government created jobs for the Irish to help them during the famine. The jobs were badly paid, hard labour on senseless projects. The Irish workers, including women and children, were given tasks like breaking stones. Then they were told to use the stones to build roads. Roads that no one wanted, leading to nowhere in particular. In the bitter winter of 1846-7 these half-starved workers were weakened by the cold and died. Some towns reported 100 to 150 dying each day. All for the few pennies they were paid. Soup kitchens were set up, but they had to be paid for by the Irish towns who were given no money to help.

"Didn't anyone care?" her brother asked.

Laura sighed. "Here. One last piece. It says 'See Lord John Russell'."

"Who was he?"

"British Prime Minister at the time," Laura said and found the item.

Russell tried to appeal for help from Parliament for the Irish. On March 23 1846 he said, "We have made Ireland the most miserable and degraded country in the world. All the world is crying shame on us but we are cruel in our disgrace and in our failure to govern." His appeal was largely ignored. Parliament was more concerned with wars abroad.

"What were they?" Ian asked.

His sister shut the computer down. "That's another problem for another day. I've done tonight's homework for you. Now I'll do my own."

"Aren't you cooking tea?" the boy asked.

"What do you want?" she asked softly. "Potatoes?"

Road of funerals — FACTS

1. Ever since the days of Oliver Cromwell the British government had interfered with Ireland's trade economy. They put controls on income made from trade by Irish farmers. When the Irish tried to rebel against British rule in their country in 1798 the British government abolished the Irish government and ruled the country from London. On 1 January 1801 the Act of Union gave Britain control over Ireland. When the Irish potato crops failed in the middle of the 19th Century, tenant farmers could not afford to pay the exceptionally large rents charged by the landlords – many of whom were English and living outside of Ireland. Seemingly oblivious to the terrible hardship they were causing by their financial demands, they insisted that the rents be paid. If they were not, the farmers and their families were removed from their homes. So not only was a large part of the population starving to death, they were rapidly becoming homeless as well.

2. There were 8.5 million alive in Ireland in 1845. By the end of the famine a million had died from starvation or disease. A further million had left the country to find a new life in North America. So a quarter of the country's population either died or emigrated. These are numbers similar to those claimed by a plague like the Black Death.

3. *Even before the famine Ireland was a poor country. A traveller at the time named Thomas Carlyle observed, "Never have I seen such beggars in the world. I often get in a rage at the beggars storming around me, like starving dogs around the remains of a dead animal. My pity changes to stony misery and disgust at the sight of such waste."*

4. *A British priest wrote in the* London Times *newspaper about the sufferings of the Irish. He was stupid enough, and cruel enough, to suggest that there were too many people in Ireland anyway. The famine would help to reduce the numbers in the country and improve life for the survivors!*

5. *One eyewitness to the suffering was an Irish magistrate. He wrote to* The Times *newspaper in 1847. He had looked into a hut and described what he saw: "Six ghastly and famished skeletons were huddled in a corner. Their only covering seemed to be a ragged horse cloth. I approached with horror and found, by a low moaning sound, that they were alive. They were in a fever. Four children, a woman and what had once been a man. In a few minutes I was surrounded by two hundred such people, such ghastly spectres that no words can describe."*

6. *Many Irish tried to escape the famine by sailing to America. There were plenty of ships to take them as America and England had a huge trade in cotton. There were as many as a thousand ships regularly taking cotton to the English mills. Those ships were*

almost empty on the trip back to America, so there was plenty of room for passengers. Unfortunately the cotton ships weren't designed to carry humans and the poor people were crowded into filthy, airless holds for the three-month voyage. Many Irish escaped the famine only to die of ship fever on their way to a new life in America.

7. *The fare was just $10 from Dublin to New York. Even the poor could afford that if they sold their belongings.*

8. *In 1807 Ireland had more people per square mile than any country in Europe. Yet so many Irish sailed to America (or died in the famine) that by the 1860s it had almost the fewest people per square mile.*

9. *Landing safe and well in America was not always the end of an Irish family's problems. They had to be accepted by America – and they could not enter the country if they were too ill or had a serious criminal record.*

4. Fire — "It wasn't me!"

Some disasters are so dramatic that they become part of history. Disasters such as the Great Fire of London of 1666 can be found in school textbooks. After months of dry weather, a small fire starts in a city of wooden houses. High winds – and a poor Fire Brigade service – allow it to spread until it destroys a large part of the city. The story of that London fire? It could be. But, in fact the reference is to the Great Chicago Fire, which happened two hundred and five years later . . .

Chicago, USA – October 1871

"Chicago Destroyed!" Hank Chestnut, the editor of the *Chicago Tribune*, tapped his teeth with a pencil. "Good headline," he said to the young reporter. "Headlines like that sell papers."

"Yes, sir," reporter Joe Kubicki nodded.

"But people in Chicago have lived through the

47

worst fire in the history of the nation. Our newspaper isn't just going to wallow in the misery and suffering."

"No sir?" Joe said and it was almost a question. He had imagined that reporting on the misery was exactly what his job was.

The editor pushed a copy of a second page across the desk towards the young man. "See what I've written for the inside pages?"

Joe read it aloud. "Chicago shall rise again."

"Know what that is?" Hank Chestnut asked.

"No, sir?"

"It's hope. That's what it is. It's their future. That's what our readers want. So throw away those stories of the deaths and the destruction. Give me the stories of the survivors!"

Joe Kubicki sifted through his notes and pulled out a sheet. "How about this, sir?"

The editor took it. Leaned back in his chair and began reading . . .

Miss Eleanor Traynor, aged about 50
The fire started on the south side of the river on Saturday, so Martha (she's my sister) and I went to take a look. We crossed the river and I said, "Praise be, Martha. We have the river between the fire and our house!"

It was a pitiable sight to be sure. People heading north, away from the flames. Some with carts piled high with their valuables, some with cases, and some just in their night-clothes. Most people had smoke-blackened faces. Seems they'd left their homes at the last moment. Our hearts went out to those poor people.

Lincoln Park looked like it had been struck by lightning. Those huge trees were just darkened stumps, still smoking.

We headed home in our carriage and it was quite frightening. Some rather rough people were trying to stop vehicles and make them go back to their homes to rescue goods. I have to say there were very few police about to help. Our driver had to strike some people back with his whip and gallop for safety! The wind was at our backs and showers of sparks were falling all around.

We arrived home that evening and retired to bed, exhausted. We heard the fire bells ringing about ten p.m. and I must confess I turned over and went back to sleep.

Then about midnight Martha woke me and said she'd never heard so many alarms! I told her not to fuss and to go back to bed. Then, at two in the morning she woke me again. "Oh, Eleanor!" she cried. "I've just looked out of the window – the fire has crossed the river to us!"

I told her that was impossible. But when I joined her at the window I had to admit those flames did seem very close. Men and women, shockingly under-dressed, were hurrying past the window from the south. I must say their screams were horrifying – and their language was not what polite ladies expect to hear!

Suddenly there was a hammering at our door. A friend from the south of the city was shouting, "Ladies! Ladies! Get up, pack your trunks and be ready to leave!"

Of course we wished to do no such thing, but I did pack a little and went to a south window to watch the red glare in the sky growing brighter. The ground below us trembled with huge explosions. I leaned out of the window and asked what was happening. It seems the mayor ordered houses to be blown up in the path of the fire. But the sparks were flying so fast and so far the idea was not working. I remembered from school history lessons that they tried this in the Fire of London. It didn't work very well then either.

"Where are the fire engines?" I cried.

"Wrecked in the blaze," someone shouted.

"The water pumping station is destroyed anyway," another added and then hurried on his way to the north and safety.

Smoke was tumbling down the street now and blotting out the moon. I decided it was time to leave. "Martha," I said. "Birds – deeds – silver – jewellery – silk dresses."

"What about them, dear?" my foolish sister asked.

"That is the order in which we must save things," I told her.

"Birds?" she said

"The canary and the parrot."

"The parrot cage is too large and heavy," she groaned.

"Then put the parrot in the canary's cage," I ordered her.

"What shall I do with the canary?" she asked.

"Set it free!" We released Lord Horatio – the canary – and he flew off through the smoke. I do fear

that the showers of sparks may have brought him down.

It was so dangerous out on that street. People were rushing down without a care for anyone else! A cart galloped down the middle and scattered people! Then it burst into flames and stopped outside our house!

We struggled with our trunks of valuables and our friend from the south helped us. But after two blocks of houses we had to abandon everything. The flames were at our backs.

I turned and looked back at St James Church. The white tower seemed to stand above the ruins all around. Then flames began to appear at the topmost windows and I watched as it fell into the inferno below.

Someone said she was my friend but I didn't know her under the soot on her face. That unknown friend gave me sips of cold tea that may well have saved my life.

I don't know how long I wandered but I remember seeing a hideous, purple face grinning down at me from the sky. I screamed. My friend told me it was only the morning sun trying to shine through the smoke.

At last we reached the shore of Lake Michigan and safety. I don't know where Martha is but I am sure she is safe. People do say there were very few deaths, though vast amounts of property have been destroyed.

My comfort comes from the story of that Great Fire of London. London was re-built a finer and a safer place. Chicago can be the same.

"A finer and a safer place," Hank Chestnut murmured. "I like that. This is the sort of stuff we want. She seems a bit of an old snob, but we'll print it!"

"Thank-you, sir," Joe Kubicki beamed.

"Anything else? Some unusual angle?"

"Plenty of those sorts of interviews, sir," the young man said sifting through his notes. "How about this one . . ."

Unknown man, aged about 30

What a fire! What a night! The best night of my life! Sure, I know 300 people died, I'm sorry about that. But they'd die sooner or late, wouldn't they? We all do!

I was in the cells below the Court House when I first heard the fire was spreading that way. A small charge of horse-stealing. I was innocent, of course. They'd arrested the wrong man with the wrong horse. Anyway, the bell in the tower above us started ringing as a warning.

We asked the warder what was going on and he told us about the fire. We were sorry to be missing the action but that's the price you pay for getting arrested.

Then we started to smell the smoke and the guys down there were getting worried. "You going to let us out?" we asked.

"Nope," the guard said. "This building is fire-proof."

The guys started to get a bit angry. 'Burning to death as a punishment has been abolished!' someone yelled. We laughed a bit at that. But an hour later we could feel the heat. That old bell stopped ringing – the ropes had burned away, they say. We were trapped under the ground and starting to fry.

At last Captain Hickey gave the order to release us. Not a minute too soon. That five-ton bell crashed from the tower, through the floors and into the basement cells just as we ran out of them.

Me and some of the guys jumped on a passing wagon and got a free ride to safety.

Me, I jumped off at a quiet street and I was passing a jeweller's shop when I thought I'd do my one good deed for the day. People were fleeing from the fire and all that jeweller's stuff would be ruined. I broke down the door and filled my pockets till I couldn't take any more. Purely as a help to the jeweller, you understand?

Then I decided to call into the nearest bar to spend some of my fortune . . . that is, I deserved a ten per-cent reward, so I decided to spend ten per-cent of the gold and jewels. When I got to the bar, would you believe it? The bar-tender was giving drinks away free! Said the bar was in direct line of the direction of the fire and beer and spirits would be lost anyway!

What a night! Escaped from jail, got a gut full of free drinks and a pocket full of jewels.

Maybe there'll be another fire next week?

The editor shook his head. "Better not use that one. Paints a bad picture of our city and its people."

"Of course, sir."

"Tell me about some others."

"Strange story of a police officer's house, sir."

"What did he do?"

"Stopped the fire at his front gate. Ripped up the

wooden sidewalk and dug a trench round his house. Filled it with a little water that he could spare. The sparks landed in it and went out. At the worst point the sparks turned the water to steam. His moat dried up and he'd run out of water."

"So what did he do?"

"Well, sir, he emptied a barrel of cider into the trench!"

"And it worked?" the editor asked.

"Oh, yes sir. His was the only house on his block to survive."

The editor closed his eyes and leaned back again. "Use that story. I can see the headline – Fire Arrested By Police Officer!"

"Very funny, sir," Joe Kubicki said with a weak smile. "There's a strange story of an undertaker hiring boys to carry his coffins to safety. The longest funeral procession Chicago's ever seen, they reckon."

"Empty coffins?"

"Er . . . not all of them, sir."

Hank Chestnut shuddered. "Bit gruesome that one. The folk who lost relatives and friends won't want to read that one."

"No, sir," the young reporter said. "I do have one very important story, sir."

The editor leaned forward and asked, "What's that, son?"

"The story of Mrs McLaughlin, sir."

"Mrs who?"

"McLaughlin, sir. Neighbour of the house where the fire started. I got the very first interview."

"Why didn't you say so? We could stop the press

for this! You'd have your story on the front page! Ever had a story on the front page?"

"I once got onto page two, sir."

"Here, let me see that . . ."

Mrs Mary McLaughlin, aged about 60

We live in the house on De Koven Street where it all started. We share the house with John and Alice O'Leary. They are a rather rough couple and we have never liked the cow they keep in a shed at the bottom of the yard.

My husband and I had been sharing a bottle of whisky with the O'Learys and about nine o'clock on Sunday evening Mrs O'Leary announced that she had to go and milk the cow. I have to say it, but she was a little the worse for the drink.

Ten minutes later she rushed back into the house – or I should say she staggered back into the house – and said the cow had kicked over the lantern and set the straw on fire.

Of course we rushed downstairs and tried to throw buckets of water over the fire. We were too late. The fire spread to the house and we just rescued a few clothes and a little money before we had to get out. They say this fire's costing two hundred million dollars. Then send the bill to Alice O'Leary, the drunken old biddy.

Great stuff, Joe. "Pity you didn't get to talk to the O'Leary woman."

"Oh, but I did, sir," he said, turning the page of his notebook. "I just don't think we can use it."

"Let me see . . ."

Alice O'Leary, aged about 55

You can't prove nothing. I never done nothing. It wasn't me. I was asleep in bed when the fire started. Don't believe a word that witch McLaughlin says. When I get my hands on her I'll rip her lying tongue out.

Hank Chestnut sighed. "I see what you mean, Joe. A lot of people are looking for someone to blame for this fire. I've heard the rumours about the O'Leary woman. I believe them . . . but we'd better not print them. It's done now. It's in the past. Let's remember the Traynor woman's words. "We'll tell our people, that Chicago can be re-built a finer and a safer place." When folk have suffered as much as our readers it's our job to offer them hope."

"Yes, sir," Joe Kubicki nodded. "I'll remember that."

"It wasn't me!" — FACTS

1. Chicago was forty years old by the time the Great Fire came. It had been built on low, swampy land and in the winter the streets became very muddy. Gravel was brought in to raise the level of the streets by 4 feet (over a metre). The houses and sidewalks were below the level of the road! And so new sidewalks were built on wooden platforms and houses were built higher. When the fire started, air was sucked under the wooden walkways, giving a wonderful supply of fresh oxygen for the flames!

2. Buildings were also lifted by huge jacks. The Great Tremont Hotel was six stories high and it was jacked up 6 feet (2 metres). Again, a dangerous air vent was left beneath it.

3. Many buildings were made of wood. Even the pumping station had a wooden roof. When the fire wrecked the pumping station roof, the pumps stopped working and Chicago was left without water to fight the fire. Even before they ran out of water the fire engines could only pump water-jets about 10 feet (3 metres) long because the wind was so strong.

4. The buildings burned fiercely because there had been such a long, dry spell of weather. Chicago had seen no rain since Independence Day, 4 July, that year. The south-westerly gales drove the fire

through the city very quickly. The fire only stopped
when it had burned a third of the city and reached
the shores of Lake Michigan. The city was re-built
quickly and continued to grow.

5. *Compare the Great Fire of Chicago with the Great*
   Fire of London two hundred years before:

	Fire of London	Fire of Chicago
Time:	2-6 Sept. 1666	8-10 Oct. 1871
Houses Lost:	13,000	17,000
People Homeless:	100,000	90,000
Deaths:	8	250
Cause:	Fire in Baker's shop	Fire in cow shed
Result:	Better, cleaner, safer city re-built	Better, cleaner, safer city re-built

5. Air crash – Dead voices

They say the safest form of travel is flying. But, when there is an air disaster it is often spectacular and frightening. In 1995 a young man went missing days before he was due to go on holiday. His family said he was terrified of flying – he was probably afraid of crashing! Maybe he knew something they didn't.

October 1930, Beauvais, France.
In 1930 some sensational headlines appeared in British newspapers . . .

1 October 1930

Avoid airship! psychic warns.

Mrs Alice Garnett, the well-known medium, has pleaded with the government to stop the test flights of two new giant airships. The successful mystic has warned that she has seen signs that spell disaster for the brave men who fly them.

The two balloons, R100 and R101, are "rigid airships" – lighter-than-air craft with a gas-filled balloon to lift the ship. Underneath the balloon is a gondola with engines to drive it through the air and space for over 100 passengers who can eat and sleep on board. The two British airships are over 700 feet long and hold 5 million cubic feet of gas. Trials having been completed, one of the airships will set off on its maiden flight to India in three days time.

Now Mrs Garnett has revealed her fears for the crew. Her first vision came in 1926, she says. "I was walking my dog in Hyde Park in London when I saw a phantom airship moving across the sky. In the past visions like that have been a warning of misfortune." She went on to explain that she had seen the phantom again in 1928, but this time it was staggering across the sky giving off smoke.

Irish-born Mrs Garnett has held seances since the 1914-18 war when she ran a hostel for wounded soldiers. She discovered she could foresee which of her returning soldiers would survive and which would die. After the war Mrs Garnett joined a group of women who wanted to contact the dead and discovered she had a talent for contacting spirits in the afterlife. Shortly after her second airship vision Mrs Garnett was contacted by the spirit of a dead airman, Raymond Hinchcliffe, with a message for a living one, Ernest Johnston, who will navigate R101. "Hinchcliffe was a friend of Johnston," Mrs Garnett explained. "He warned Johnston not to go on the maiden voyage of the new airship because it will crash."

The medium had her third vision recently. This time the phantom airship was falling in flames. She took her story to Sir Sefton Branker, Britain's Director of Civil Aviation. Sir Sefton stated, "R101 is as safe as a house – except for a freak million-to-one chance. In fact I will be joining the maiden flight to India myself."

Rigid airships are the transport of the future, the government believes. Airships have already crossed the Atlantic and flown over the North Pole. The sister ship, R100, has been to Canada and back. But Mrs Garnett is sure from her contact with the spirit of Raymond Hinchcliffe that R101 is the doomed craft. There have been a few fatal airship crashes in the past few years but Sir Sefton believes they are becoming safer all the time. "When we land in India then Mrs Garnett's gloomy fantasies will look very silly . . . and that's my prediction!"

Unfortunately the authorities refused to take any notice of Mrs Garnett's predictions and the results were disastrous . . .

6 October 1930

R101 Crashes in France

Reports are coming in from France that the British airship R101 has crashed near Beauvais. The craft was on its maiden flight to India when it came down in fields.

There were 54 crew and passengers on board, including Director of Civil Aviation, Sir Sefton Branker. First reports suggest that there were few survivors.

The Ministry of Transport is unwilling to comment on the cause of the crash. Heavy rain and strong headwinds were reported as R101 crossed the English Channel and airships are known to be difficult to steer in gales. The airship caught fire and was destroyed in the tragedy. With few survivors it is possible that the cause of the crash may never be known. A spokesman for the Ministry said that there will be a Court of Inquiry as soon as possible.

Last week the spiritualist medium, Alice Garnett, tried to warn Ministry officials that R101 was in danger. Mrs Garnett was said to be very distressed by the catastrophe and saddened that her warnings to navigator Ernest Johnston had not been taken seriously.

It didn't take long for the newspapers to discover another sensation. Three days after the first reports there was a new story to grab their attention . . .

9 October 1930

R101: Remarkable Seance

While all the world wonders what happened to the giant airship R101, the dead captain of the ship has given his own version of the crash . . . in a remarkable seance!

Last night I attended a seance at the National Laboratory of Psychical Research. The famous spiritualist and novelist, Sir Arthur Conan Doyle, died on July 7 this year. He promised to contact his friends after his death. Irish medium, Alice Garnett, held the seance in the hope of contacting Sir Arthur, the creator of Sherlock Holmes. What happened was a greater mystery than any that great detective ever had to solve!

I was present as an independent witness and took notes. Mrs Garnett went into a trance and made contact with her friendly voice in the spirit world. She asked to be put in touch with Sir Arthur but instead another voice broke through and began talking. "I must do something about it!" he said, speaking through Mrs Garnett.

"Who are you?" someone asked.

"Irwin. Flight Lieutenant Carmichael Irwin. Captain of the R101."

"What do you want to tell us?"

"About the crash. The crash of the R101. An inquiry will be held . . . it will hide the truth. I want you to know what really happened."

"Tell us," I urged, scribbling in shorthand as quickly as I could.

"The airship should never have flown . . . much too heavy for the engines driving her . . . had to dive for safety five times during the test flights . . . the public never knew that. There wasn't enough lift . . . the elevators used to jam . . . an oil pipe became plugged . . . and the engine lost power . . . the load was too great for a long flight . . . too slow and we had to fly too low."

"What happened on the India flight?" someone asked.

"Bad weather . . . heading into a gale . . . pouring rain."

"So why did you set off?" I asked. "Why didn't you wait for the weather to clear?"

"Crew decided to risk it. Didn't want to seem like a bunch of cowards. Crossed the English Channel slowly but safely. But that wind grew stronger. We decided to land at Le Bourget airport. At least they can't say we didn't try. The whole balloon was twisting when we hit the gales. One of the girders in the balloon cracked. It punctured the balloon. We lost gas. The rain soaked into the balloon fabric. Made it too heavy. The extra weight and the gas leak drove us down. The engines weren't powerful enough to lift us back up. We scraped roof tops at the village of Achy. Tried to follow the railway line."

Suddenly the voice switched to describing the accident as if it was happening there and then. "The gas pressure gauge is going up and down now . . . we're losing height . . . air pump faulty . . . fuel pump sticking . . . what was that bang? The gas valve's blown clean off . . . gas escaping over engines . . . just one backfire and the gas will explode . . . just like SL8 . . . try to get us down, engineer . . . that's it! We're on fire! We're finished! When we hit the ground it's every man for himself . . . jump and run for it. I'll stay at the controls as long as possible. Open the safety hatches. Get out! Get out! The fire . . . the heat . . . we're finished . . ."

Mrs Garnett gasped and went silent. A minute or two later she came out of her trance. We repeated what she had said in her trance. She has promised to try to contact other dead crew members – even Sir Sefton Branker, Britain's Director of Civil Aviation who died in the crash having ignored the medium's warning.

Meanwhile the authorities at the airship base in Cardington are refusing to comment on the evidence from the seance. An official would only say, "It is nonsense to say that the R101 was faulty. We would not have sent 54 men on the voyage, knowing that the airship was unsafe. There will be a court inquiry and the truth will come out at that."

Mrs Garnett's evidence was very convincing, however. The British public will be asking the Ministry of Civil Aviation some very hard questions about their part in the crash.

This reporter will keep *Morning Post* readers informed of future seance revelations.

When the inquiry met the following year, the newspapers had not forgotten the supernatural happenings surrounding the crash . . .

18 March 1931

R101 – seance rejected.

The inquiry into last year's R101 airship disaster is refusing to listen to evidence from spiritualists who have spoken to the dead captain and crew of the ill-fated craft. The inquiry opened today with expert technical witnesses giving their verdicts on possible causes. However, the chairman of the hearing ruled that, "Evidence from the dead could not be allowed in an English court of law."

Famous Irish medium, Mrs Alice Garnett, said she was disappointed that the truth may never be told. Since speaking to the spirit of R101 captain, Carmichael Irwin, Mrs Garnett and her team of spiritualists have contacted other members of the crew. Some of the information she has gathered has proved amazingly accurate. Some facts were known to only the crew and a few experts at the Cardington base. How could Mrs Garnett have discovered these facts if she wasn't truly speaking to the dead crew? This amazing woman:

- Gave technical information on the new hydrogen-carbon fuel mix which was top secret at the time
- Pinpointed the village of Achy as being near the crash site – a village so small it was only found by investigators using detailed map charts of the kind carried on the airship
- Used technical terms such as gas pressure gauge unknown to her before
- Mentioned strange phrases which only an experienced airship captain would know – the reference to SL8 puzzled everyone. Finally our expert from Cardington airbase tracked it down as the code name of a war-time German airship, shot down over England in 1916

Mrs Garnett has been questioned (in a trance) by Major Oliver Villiers of the Ministry of Civil Aviation. Major Villiers was a close friend of Director Sir Sefton Branker who perished in the tragedy. He backs the medium's claims. "If her secret knowledge is so accurate, then why shouldn't the inquiry listen to her?" he said yesterday.

The *Morning Post* asks, "What is the government afraid of?"

Dead Voices — FACTS

Did Alice Garnett really talk to the spirits of the victims? Newspapers of the 1930s made a lot of fuss about the Alice Garnett seances. Later ghost investigators said that the seances prove there is life after death. Books have been written about the case which try to show that Alice Garnett was more accurate with her spirit information than the judges in the inquiry were with their findings. It is true that she "saw" the disaster and warned the Director ten days before the R101 crashed. But we have to be more careful about the newspaper claims for her spirit conversations. Here are some facts the newspapers of the time did not print:-

1. The building of the R101 was not as secret as the newspapers tried to make out. Anyone could have found out about its new hydrogen-carbon fuel mix.

2. The village of Achy was near the crash site – but it is very unlikely that R101 passed over the top of it and brushed the houses. Alice Garnett often drove from Calais to Paris. A signpost points quite clearly to Achy village. It is no mystery, then, that the name stuck in her mind.

3. Some of the special terms such as gas pressure gauge sounded very technical. In fact, engineers who worked on the R101 pointed out that there was no such thing as a gas pressure gauge.

4. The SL8 accident happened just 14 years before the R101 tragedy. It was reported in all the newspapers and was not a rare piece of information. The so-called "expert" from Cardington Airship Works was simply a construction worker called Charlton. He was no expert and proved it when he said he had no idea what SL8 stood for until he looked it up. The mention of SL8 didn't actually prove how much Mrs Garnett knew – it proved how little Charlton knew.

5. The airship did not catch fire and crash, as Alice Garnett's voice said . . . it crashed and then caught fire. A central girder did not snap and puncture the side of the balloon as her spirits claimed.

No one has suggested that Mrs Garnett was a liar or a fraud. But the R101 case was covered in all of the newspapers of the day. It would not be surprising if she read all the papers, stored all the information and had it on her mind when she went into the trance.

Why did R101 crash?

1. The two airships were built as a competition – the best design would be used for a future fleet of airships. R100 was built by a private company, Vickers; R101 was built by the government's company at Cardington, at a cost of £1 million to taxpayers. R100 was fast, light and safe – R101 had to fly at any cost to prove the money was well spent. That "cost" proved to be 48 lives.

2. *The balloon was constructed from the skin linings of a million ox-intestines. R101 was filled with hydrogen gas, which is explosive. Experts said that helium gas would have worked just as well. The government decided that they would use the more dangerous hydrogen gas because it was cheaper.*

3. *R101 was much heavier than its rival R100, because it used larger diesel engines and huge power-steering machinery. Its gas bags moved in flight and rubbed against the steel frame. Holes soon wore through and gas escaped at over 1,000 cubic feet an hour. Designers tried to cure the problem by cutting the balloon in two and putting in an extra 40-foot section so it would hold more gas. In fact, they made it weaker.*

4. *The government insisted that the first flight would happen in October – whether the airship was safe or not. The new governor of India wanted to fly to that country in style and couldn't wait. The air safety inspector said it was dangerous. He wrote a report to the government which was mysteriously "lost". The safety certificate was granted – minutes before the airship took off.*

5. *R101 set out in dreadful weather. The front covering of the balloon tore off when it reached France, the nose went down and the airship hit the top of a hill. Six crew were thrown clear and survived. No fire service in the world could have put out the hydrogen fire once it started.*

6. Volcano — Monstrous mountain

Take all the plants and creatures off this planet and the Earth would still be "alive". It moves and shapes itself as it spins through space. Its forces are immense, so when it moves its human passengers had better beware. Sometimes there is violence without warning.

Mount St Helens, USA – May 1980

Somewhere, deep beneath the ground, something stirred. It had been sleeping for years. It was a giant of awesome power; humans would be blown away like butterflies on the breath of a dragon. It stirred, it stretched and the earth above trembled . . .

Harry Truman was kneeling at the graveside of his wife Edna when he felt that first stirring. "Well, Edna, did you feel that? Seems like our old friend is waking up, eh? But don't worry, I'll not leave you. Not now."

He rose and looked up at the mountain. He was eighty-four years-old and as tough as that mountain.

His denims were faded and worn, his skin was like old leather, but those eyes – bluer than Spirit Lake that stretched behind him and sharper than the mountain deer's. The mountain deer felt the trembling earth too and began to run.

Harry wasn't afraid. Harry wasn't running for anyone or anything. Not even the monster under the mountain.

The monster breathed. Its hot gases broke through the crust of its mountain home. Steam hissed as it escaped through the top of the mountain. Hot ashes blew through a crater in the top. They settled on the side of the snowy slopes and stained them charcoal grey.

The sides of the mountain began to crack. When the monster breathed the rest of the world held its own breath. In the forests and on the farms and in the cities they waited nervously.

And then the monster slept and the people could once more relax. Except for the brave ones who set off to investigate this dragon in its lair.

David Johnston. A brilliant scientist. Like all great scientists he possessed one quality above all others: curiosity. The chance to study an active volcano was too great an opportunity to miss.

He arrived in a house trailer and parked six miles from Mount St Helens. Each day he was flown in by helicopter to take samples. "We test the ash for the minerals in it," he explained to his pilot. "From that we can tell how big the explosion's going to be."

"You think it'll be a big one?" the pilot asked.

72

"Oh we're sure it'll be a monster. The trouble is it's like sitting next to a barrel of gunpowder. We know how big the bang will be when it goes off . . . but we don't know how long the fuse is. We don't know when it'll blow. Another month, another hour maybe?"

"Now he tells me," the pilot muttered as he hovered over the bubbling, fuming, boiling crater.

Harry Truman tried to explain to the deputy sheriff: "I've lived here fifty years. That old mountain's my friend. Why, I've heard her tremble a hundred or more times," he said. "She's never hurt me yet."

"Mr Truman," the young officer said patiently. "You may have lived through earth tremors. But you've never lived here when the volcano actually erupted."

"Hell, no! The last time was 1857! Even I'm not that old!" the old man laughed.

"That's why we're ordering all residents to leave the area now, sir," the sheriff went on.

The old man's mood changed. "No one orders me off my own land," he said. "My life's here. Edna and me, we swore years ago we'd never leave Spirit Lake. I love it like it's part of me . . . and I'm part of that mountain. If that mountain drove me out then I wouldn't live a week anyway – probably not even a day. Edna left our house feet first. And that's the only way I'm going to leave it, understand?"

"Yes, sir, but . . ."

Harry wasn't listening to him. He was sitting on his front porch watching the waters of Spirit Lake. Watching and remembering. "We built the house with our own hands fifty years ago. Then we built cabins so folk could come up here for a vacation or just to go fishing. A good business it was too. When Edna died three years ago I gave up renting the cabins. Just allow a little fishing in the summer. You saw that steel gate across the road as you came up?"

"Yes, sir," the deputy sheriff nodded.

"The state put that up ten years ago to keep people out – 'conservation' they said. They also locked me in! That didn't drive me out. I'm having a fine time living on my own. Plenty of whisky . . . enough food to last to my hundredth birthday I reckon. Got it all stored in an old mine shaft. If that old mountain blows its top then that's where you'll find me."

The monster stirred again. Six times in as many weeks. It seemed to half-waken then fall asleep again. But that was only on the outside. Deep in its heart the pressure was building up. When it did break out then it would be with a force that would tear the top off the mountain.

David Johnston wiped sweat from his brow. He'd gone down further than ever into the smoking pit, snatched his samples from the jaws of the wakening monster and run back laughing.

"I wish you wouldn't go down so far, Mr Johnston," the pilot said as the scientist climbed back onto the helicopter. "I can smell you burning!"

David grinned. "That's just the tip of my beard. It's nothing."

"But if it blows while you're down there . . ."

"That's a chance I'll have to take. I promise I'll run

for my life . . . you know that's why I was chosen for this job? Because my hobby is running marathon races," he explained.

"This time the opposition isn't some feller in trainers and a vest," the pilot grumbled.

David saw the worry on the man's face. He became serious again. "I don't want to risk your life," he said.

"So you won't go back?"

"No . . . what I'm saying is watch for the first signs of trouble. If you see something – anything – that scares you I want you to take off. Leave me. Let the risk be mine."

The reporter trudged up the dusty, rutted road to Harry Truman's lodge. Her shoes would be fine in the city. Here they made her stumble as her ankles twisted with every other step.

Harry Truman watched her from the porch and laughed. "Have a whisky and ice. I've been watching you come up that road. Reckon you need it."

"Thanks, Mr Truman," she panted as she took the glass from him and sank to the chair that faced Spirit Lake.

"What can I do for you now, eh?" the man asked.

"Mr Truman, do you know how famous you're becoming? I published your story in *The Seattle Times* and everyone admires the way you're staying here."

Harry stroked one of the dozen cats that wandered through his house. "I've been getting letters since your last visit," he admitted. "Some of them are just plain crazy. People want to rescue me! Don't they understand? I could rescue myself now . . . if that's what I wanted?"

"You could come back with me now," the woman said eagerly. What a story that would be!

Harry ignored the suggestion. "I get letters from people who want to save my soul. One of them sent me a Bible!" he threw back his head and laughed, then reached down to pick up a handful of letters from the floor beside him. "Now these letters . . . these are proposals of marriage! Imagine that? Some of the kids are eighteen years old. Did you ever hear of such a thing?"

The reporter managed a smile. "None of the letters change your mind?" she asked.

The old man picked up a big bundle. "I wouldn't say that. These here are from a school in Oregon. Not just a few kids or a class . . . the whole school. Want to know all about me and my mountain," he said. "I can't reply to all of them!"

"You could if you went to visit them," the reporter said quickly. "Let me use your phone and I'll arrange it for you. My paper will fly you down by helicopter . . . if we can have the exclusive story."

Harry looked at the letters in his hand for a long time. Finally he sniffed and said, "You know, I'd like that. I think I'd like that!"

David was worried by the reports. "We took heat-image pictures last time we flew over," he told his pilot. "They showed there was a hot spot on the side of the mountain. I want to take a look at the north-west ridge today."

The pilot nodded and swung the helicopter towards the site the scientist showed him on the map. "Why is that so interesting?" he asked.

"Most volcanoes blow through the crater in the top. No one's ever seen one blow through the side. We don't know what the effect will be," David explained.

"I hope you don't find out the hard way," his pilot sighed.

"What would you do if you saw the lava coming to get you?" a wide-eyed girl asked Harry Truman.

"I'd run faster than a tom-cat with a tiger on its tail!" he answered.

The hundred-and-four children giggled and looked at him adoringly. He'd given them each a postcard picture of Spirit Lake and his lodge. He'd signed each one and they held the pictures as carefully as you would a kitten.

"Please, Mister Truman," a shy boy stammered. "When the ground shakes, how do you keep from falling out of bed?"

"Glad you asked me that, young man. I wear my boots in bed and tie the laces to the bedposts!"

The children roared with laughter. It took them a minute or so to settle again. The teacher, Mr Thorson, raised a hand and said, "You've been answering all the children's questions for over an hour. You must be getting tired. Can I finish with one last question. What's it like to live in the same place for fifty years?"

Harry nodded his head slowly and dropped his joking voice. "I recommend it. I always remember that girl Dorothy in *The Wizard of Oz*. She said something like, 'You can travel all over the world, but there's really no place like home.' That's how I feel about Spirit Lake. Lived there as long as I can remember – probably die there one day." He sensed the sadness in the children and his face cracked into a crooked grin. "But not for another hundred years I guess!"

The children laughed. That would be their memory of him. The laughter of a funny and stubborn old man. As his helicopter rose from the school playing fields he looked back at the banner that the waving children had unrolled. In huge letters it said simply, "We love you Harry!"

The pilot knocked on the door of David Johnston's cabin. "You flying today, Mr Johnston."

The scientist shook his head. "They've measured the earthquake force today. The volcano can't take much more. It'll blow any time. I want to see it, of course, but I reckon this six miles is the closest I'll get."

The pilot blew out his cheeks. "I'm pleased, Mr Johnston. I thought you might try once too often."

The young scientist laughed. "I don't have a death wish. I've seen most of what I came to see. I want this thing to blow. Then I can get back home to my wife. We've not long been married."

The pilot pulled his cap on and said, "Best of luck."

When the monster broke out of its slumber it was with a fury that no one expected. It broke through the side with a roar of gas that was heard two hundred miles away. Not upwards into the atmosphere – but sideways into the woods with a force that flattened the forest like a cornfield in a storm.

The blast rushed out at the speed of an aircraft. Then the ash. A thick, suffocating, scorching breath of wind from the heart of the Earth.

Then the north wall collapsed. The top was blown off Mount St Helens. Boulders were lifted like dust, then thrown like rain upon the ground. The grey cloud of smoke smothered the sun and blotted out the light. The heat caused thunder-storms to crackle and flare through the blackness.

The end of the world cannot look more like a nightmare than those first hours of the Mount St Helens disaster.

David Johnston reached his radio. "Vancouver! Vancouver!" he called excitedly. "This is it . . ." Six miles should have been a safe distance. But that first blast shot out sideways. It covered the six miles in ten seconds. His travelling home was thrown off the ridge and over Coldwater Creek. His body was never found.

Some people believed that old Harry Truman may have reached the safety of his mine shaft with his fifteen years' supply of food.

As the days, then weeks, then years passed, they knew he'd never be seen again. His precious lodge was buried under the cinder-hard ash from the mountain he loved. The falling mountain top filled his favourite lake and made the level rise till it flooded his home. Home sweet home. His home for the rest of time.

Monstrous mountain — Facts

The 1980 eruption of Mount St Helens killed sixty-one people – even though everyone knew it was going to happen. The spectacle of an erupting volcano seemed to draw a lot of people towards it rather than frighten them away. Photographers and artists, tourists and scientists all wanted a closer look. Many died as a result of their curiosity. The mistake was to believe that they were safe at a distance of ten miles – four foresters died in the first blast and they were fourteen miles away. The eruption when it arrived destroyed 200 square miles of forest.

1. Not only did the heat and blast of the eruption cause damage. Because of the way the eruption blew the top off the mountain it was shortened from 2950 metres to 2550 metres. That is 400 metres of mountain sliding down to change the whole landscape for ever. It blocked rivers and caused them to flood. The falling dust choked car and aircraft engines so that emergency services struggled to reach victims. Cities hundreds of miles away from Mount St Helens were coated with black dust – pavements, roof-tops, cars and anyone caught out in the open. When the rains came it turned to a filthy sludge.

2. Winds carried the ash across most of the United States in three days. Within seventeen days the dust had gone all the way round the world. Scientists

said that where the dust fell on the farms the soil would become much richer. Volcanic ash is a good fertiliser.

3. Native American Indians knew about the force of Mount St Helens. A legend grew around the mountain. It said that two warriors fought over a beautiful maiden. They hurled fiery rocks at each other. The Great Spirit was so upset that he turned the warriors – and the maiden – into mountains. Mount St Helens was one.

7. The Sea — "Why am I here?"

When a disaster is human-made, then people usually look for someone in particular to blame – anyone. Disasters are rarely that simple. And the guilt that the person blamed suffers can destroy their life. They often wish the disaster had killed them too – even when they have behaved heroically . . .

The North Atlantic Ocean – September 1854
First the calm. Then the panic. Then the shameful cowardice.

I woke in the hospital sobbing. "Why am I here?" I asked again and again. "Why was I saved when all the rest are lost?"

A nurse took a damp towel and wiped my forehead. She checked my pulse and pushed my head back onto the pillows. "Hush, Captain Luce," she said. "There's nothing you can do about it now. You're alive."

"I'd rather be dead," I told her.

"You are just feeling sorry for yourself," she said sharply.

She was wrong. That was not the pitiful whine of a hollow man. I meant it from the bottom of my heart.

Listen and tell me how you would feel.

I was Captain of the paddle steamer *Arctic*, sailing from London to Newfoundland. A trip I'd done dozens of times before. By September 27 we were just forty miles off the Newfoundland coast when I went on deck to calculate our position. The sea was flat calm but there were patches of fog. "Should we reduce speed, Captain Luce?" the mate, Francis Dorian asked.

"No. Steady full speed ahead," I told him. He was a good man. I had to make do with a crew of idle and grumbling sailors, but Dorian was a man I'd pick every time. As well as being good at his job, he also got on well with my son, Edward.

I was sitting at my charts two minutes later when I heard the cry, "Hard to starboard! Ship dead ahead!"

I felt a slight shudder as we struck the other ship. When I reached the deck, seconds later, I saw her. A French steamer, the *Vesta*. It looked as if we'd taken the whole of her bow away. "Send a lifeboat to her aid," I ordered. It seemed she would sink in minutes.

We began to circle the *Vesta* and it was pitiful to see the people rush to her decks and scramble for places in her lifeboats. Many fell overboard in the panic and drowned in the cruel, cold sea.

My eight-year-old son Edward stood beside me on the deck. "Why are they fighting?" he asked.

"I don't know, son. There is a rule at sea that if a

ship starts to sink then the women and the children should be helped to safety first," I explained.

"I wouldn't go without you," he said seriously.

"That's because you are a man," I said proudly.

What is it they say? Pride goes before a fall? And there is a calm that goes before a storm.

First came the calm.

Francis Dorian came on deck and said quietly, "Captain Luce, sir, we are taking on water."

"Much?"

"Enough."

"Has anyone inspected the damage?"

"There are a few holes in our bow, just below the water line. The water's coming in faster than the pumps can empty it."

"Cover it with a sail," I said. Calm, so calm.

The *Arctic* was becoming difficult to handle and we'd drifted off course. We lost the *Vesta* in the fog.

I walked quickly down the steps to the engine room and gave the crew their orders. "We'll make a run for Cape Ace," I said. "Have all the pumps working. We should reach land before we sink."

Chief Stoker Manning was an ox of a man. Red-faced from the heat of the boilers and with a beard that almost covered his bare chest. "Maybe we should launch the lifeboats now," he said.

Some of his stokers began to mutter in agreement. That was the end of the calm and the start of the panic. I thought my calm could swallow that panic. My pride was wrong again. "The women and children go first," I told them. "We have four hundred passengers on this ship. We have a duty to them first."

85

"And I've got a wife back in Liverpool, Captain," Manning spat. "I have a duty to her."

"If you give us full speed we'll be ashore in two hours," I told him. I turned to the men. "And if you work those pumps, then no one will need to take to the lifeboats."

I turned and trotted back on deck. Dorian waited for me at the top of the stairs. A half-drowned man sat on the deck with a blanket wrapped around him. "Where did he come from?" I asked.

"The *Vesta*, Captain. This man was rescued by the lifeboat we launched to help them."

"We've picked up the lifeboat?" I said.

"Not exactly," the mate sighed. "We ran over it in the fog. Smashed it to splinters. This man is the only survivor."

"Take care of him," I said. The chances of hitting the *Vesta* must have been a million to one. The chances of hitting our own small lifeboat in that huge ocean? I'd have said it was impossible. But when fate decides to crush you it will do the impossible.

Passengers were beginning to crowd the deck of the *Arctic* by now. That ripple of panic was starting to run through them. "I will have our five lifeboats made ready," I announced. "I don't expect we'll need them, but perhaps the women and children would like to form an orderly queue at each boat?"

I felt a faint touch at my side. Edward stood beside me. A calm island in the swelling sea of fear.

By my calculation we had covered twelve of the forty miles in the first hour. Then the ship gave a shudder, steam instead of smoke poured from the funnel . . . men poured from below the decks. Angry men carrying bottles. It seems they'd broken into the liquor store. Manning led them.

"You should be manning the pumps," I said.

"The water's swamped the boiler," Manning growled. "We've no steam for the engines and no steam for the pumps. The only place this ship is going is to the bottom of the ocean."

Someone cried in fear. The wails of despair grew. "Women and children first!" I called over the noise.

"Take that lifeboat!" Manning roared to his followers.

The stokers ran to the first boat and began to lower it into the sea.

One woman, braver than the others, rushed at him and began to pull at his arms as strong as anchor cables. He threw her off viciously and she stumbled until she hit the rail and fell over. Her sharp scream was cut off suddenly when she hit that cold water.

The others huddled together, helpless, and could only watch as the stokers lowered a lifeboat. I stepped forward and ordered the rest of the crew to stand clear of the four remaining lifeboats.

Engineer Whittle reached into his jacket and pulled out a revolver. "Crew first, Captain. Stand back or I blow your brains out . . . then I blow out the brains of your little boy. Either way we live."

"The women . . ." I began to protest.

"Oh yes, the wives and daughters of the rich. Well let their money save them," he sneered and turned to join his men in the boat.

Then the panic. My voice was lost in the screaming

and the praying and the shouting. There was a new rule on the *Arctic* now: the strongest first. First the crew took the boats, then the men passengers.

The ship was tilting towards the stern. Of the officers, only Mate Francis Dorian remained. He was making sure every woman and child had a life-belt. He called from the bows, "A raft, Captain Luce. It's our best chance!"

He was right. There was plenty of wood, rope and canvas on the *Arctic*. In the half hour or less that we had left, we should be able to lash together a life-raft.

Some who stayed calm enough were able to help. When it was finished there was no need for us to launch it – the ship began to slip quickly below the water and the raft launched itself.

I scrambled up to the bridge of the ship, only too glad to be going down with it. If the evil of that crew was to survive in the world then I did not want to be part of it. As the raft began to float, the remaining men barged their way onto it. Women and children were tumbled into the sea and dragged down by the weight of their heavy dresses.

I searched for my son but could not see him. Then a quiet voice behind me said, "I am here, father. I said I'd go down with you."

I clutched him to me as the cold water began sucking at our ankles. The last thing I heard before the water rushed over our heads was the sobbing of the women.

The grey of the water turned to midnight blue, the deeper we sank. Still I clung to my son and waited to die. I closed my eyes. Light began to force its way through my eyelids and I realised we were drifting back to the surface.

We choked on the foaming surface. The *Arctic* loomed above us. I knew that when it finally vanished it would create a whirlpool that would suck us down with it. We were going to have to die a second time.

The paddles on the side of the ship were covered by a large wooden case. As it floated past, the case broke away and crashed down on us. It struck Edward on the head and swept him out of my arms. His end must have been mercifully quick. But that was when I first gave the cry that has haunted me ever since. "Why am I here?"

The paddle box that killed my son saved me. It floated and I struggled onto it with ten other men.

The next two days are a dream that I want to forget. When the seas began to rise, the frozen men were torn from the box one by one.

There was the terrible thirst and hunger.

Then a second storm and men swept away two by two. Still death refused to take me.

After two days we were pulled aboard a Canadian ship. Three of us. We had all lost our families aboard the *Arctic*. We were not three men happy to be alive – we were three corpses, walking the world, eating sleeping and breathing – able to feel the pain of our loss – but unable to die.

When they put me in this hospital I had visitors. There was the owner of the shipping line, Edward Knight Collins.

"I lost my wife and children on that ship," he said.

"Your son was one of the few brave crewmen," I

said to console him. Coit Collins had stayed at the distress gun, firing it every minute in the hope of being heard through the fog. He was firing it when the *Arctic* went down.

Mr Collins stared at me with eyes as cold as that sea. "I blame you, Captain Luce. I blame you for the accident and I blame you for allowing the disgraceful behaviour of your crew."

I said, "I tried to save the women with a life-raft."

"They say seventy-two men crowded onto that raft and just four women. They were more in than out of the water. As the cold gripped them the women were the first to go. Then the men went. When the Canadians found it there was just one man on it, Captain Luce. Your life-raft saved just one life."

"The women and children. How many lived?"

He took a deep breath. "Ah, yes. Women and children first, isn't that the rule? There were two hundred aboard the *Arctic* – and two hundred men. Eighty-seven men survived – eighty of those were your crew, Captain Luce."

I felt the shame and the blame. "The women?" I cried.

"Oh, they are easier to count. Not one woman or child survived, Captain Luce. Not one." He walked to my bedside and cut me with his eyes. "I will make sure you never captain another ship as long as you live, Luce," he said, and his heels cracked hard on the tiled floor as he marched out.

"Why am I here?" I asked the nurse.

"You are just feeling sorry for yourself," she said.

"Why am I here?" — FACTS

1. The disgraceful behaviour of the Arctic crew
   shocked people in Britain and the United States.
   Five lifeboats reached Canada and every one was
   filled with men – mostly the Arctic's crew. The
   majority of these men chose to stay in Canada
   rather than face the anger of the Americans or
   British back home. There were also ten people,
   including Captain Luce, who had managed to
   survive by clinging to wreckage.

2. The owner of the shipping line, Edward Knight
   Collins, lost his wife and two children in the
   disaster and the President of the company, James
   Brown, lost six children and grandchildren. The
   Collins ships were not so popular after the sinking
   of the Arctic. When the ship Pacific vanished a year
   later, with the loss of 288 lives, the Atlantic
   passengers lost all confidence in the company. It
   was not only Captain Luce who suffered the jinx
   that seemed to hang over the Collins ships. Luce
   lost his son and his job – Collins lost his family and
   his business.

3. Amazingly, the ship that collided with the Arctic,
   the Vesta, stayed afloat and managed to get back to
   port with very few losses. After this accident the
   United States Navy came up with a scheme for
   shipping "lanes". A series of maps showed how
   east-bound and west-bound vessels could travel

*along different paths – like cars on a motorway –
and not be in danger of colliding. The deaths of the
passengers on the* Arctic *led to this idea, which
probably saved thousands of lives in the next
hundred years. The shipping "lanes" idea is still in
use today.*

4. *The worst recorded sea disaster was the sinking of
the ferry* Dona Paz. *It collided with a tanker off the
Philippines: 4,386 people died.*

5. *The most famous disaster was probably the sinking
of the* Titanic *in 1912. 1,403 people died when this
"unsinkable" liner struck an iceberg in the
Atlantic. As she left harbour, her huge size
"sucked" two smaller ships towards her. They
almost collided. If they had crashed into the* Titanic
*then the liner would have had to stop her voyage
for repairs. She would never have then struck that
iceberg. In escaping a small accident, the* Titanic
*went on to a much greater disaster. Just as Captain
Luce was accused of reckless speed in the fog, the
Captain of the* Titanic, *Commander Edward J.
Smith, was accused of going too fast after warnings
of icebergs. However, there was one great
difference between the sinking of the* Titanic *and
that of the* Arctic. *The behaviour of the passengers
and crew. Many people on the* Titanic *were true
heroes and kept their dignity in the face of the
danger . . .*

• *76% of the 439 women on board survived, because*

92

the rule "women and children first" was stuck to. 50% of the 105 children survived but only 19% of the 1,662 men lived.

- *Even more women and children would have been saved but some refused to leave their husbands or fathers and chose to die with them.*
- *There were 84 men on the stokehold watch of the crew. They were safely on deck but went below a dangerous second time to keep the boilers going. Only eight were saved.*
- *There were 36 engineers in the crew – they kept the engines running until 3 minutes before the ship sank, so that there would be light for the rescuers. Not one of the engineers was saved.*
- *There were 5 postal clerks. They worked steadily to save the mail, though the postal room was flooded early on. Not one of the postal clerks was saved.*
- *There were an unknown number of ship's boys. They helped load the boats and make sure passengers had biscuits for their comfort in the lifeboats. Not one of the ship's boys was saved.*
- *Commander Edward J. Smith was reported to have died on his ship crying out, "Be British!" Other reports speak of him swimming in the sea trying to save the life of a child. He was not saved.*
- *There were eight players in the ship's band. They played dance music to relax the passengers as they climbed into the lifeboats. As the water flowed around their feet, the band played a final hymn. Then there was silence. None of the eight musicians was saved.*